I0417429

science for a changing world

National Assessment of Hurricane-Induced Coastal Erosion Hazards: Southeast Atlantic Coast

By Hilary F. Stockdon, Kara J. Doran, David M. Thompson, Kristin L. Sopkin, and Nathaniel G. Plant

Open-File Report 2013–1130

U.S. Department of the Interior
U.S. Geological Survey

U.S. Department of the Interior
SALLY JEWELL, Secretary

U.S. Geological Survey
Suzette M. Kimball, Acting Director

U.S. Geological Survey, Reston, Virginia 2013

This report and any updates to it are available online at:
http://pubs.usgs.gov/of/2013/1130/

For more information on the USGS—the Federal source for science about the Earth,
its natural and living resources, natural hazards, and the environment—visit *http://www.usgs.gov*
or call 1-888-ASK-USGS

For an overview of USGS information products, including maps, imagery, and publications,
visit *http://www.usgs.gov/pubprod*

To order this and other USGS information products, visit *http://store.usgs.gov*

Suggested citation:
Stockdon, H.F., Doran, K.J., Thompson, D.M., Sopkin, K.L., and Plant, N.G., 2013, National assessment of hurricane-induced coastal erosion hazards: Southeast Atlantic Coast: U.S. Geological Survey Open-File Report 2013-1130, 28 p.

Contents

Figures

Tables

Conversion Factors

SI to Inch/Pound

Multiply	By	To obtain
Length		
centimeter (cm)	0.3937	inch (in.)
millimeter (mm)	0.03937	inch (in.)
meter (m)	3.281	foot (ft)
kilometer (km)	0.6214	mile (mi)
kilometer (km)	0.5400	mile, nautical (nmi)
meter (m)	1.094	yard (yd)
Flow rate		
meter per second (m/s)	2.237	mile per hour (mi/h)

Vertical coordinate information is referenced to the North American Vertical Datum of 1988 (NAVD 88)
Horizontal coordinate information is referenced to the North American Datum of 1983 (NAD 83).

Abbreviations

CHARTS	Compact Hydrographic Airborne Rapid Total Survey
CRM	Coastal Relief Model
DEM	digital elevation model
EAARL	Experimental Advanced Airborne Research Lidar
GPS	Global Positioning System
HWL	High Water Line
Hz	Hertz
IPCC	Intergovernmental Panel on Climate Change
Lidar	Light Detection and Ranging
MHW	Mean High Water
MOM	maximum of the maximum
NAD83	North American Datum 1983
NAVD88	North American Vertical Datum 1988
NGDC	National Geophysical Data Center
NGVD29	National Geodetic Vertical Datum 1929
NHC	National Hurricane Center
NOAA	National Oceanic and Atmospheric Administration

RMS	Root-Mean-Square
SLOSH	Sea, Lake, and Overland Surges from Hurricanes
SWAN	Simulating WAves Nearshore
USACE	U.S. Army Corps of Engineers
USGS	U.S. Geological Survey
WIS	Wave Information Studies

National Assessment of Hurricane-Induced Coastal Erosion Hazards: Southeast Atlantic Coast

By Hilary F. Stockdon, Kara S. Doran, David M. Thompson, Kristin L. Sopkin, and Nathaniel G. Plant

1. Introduction

1.1 Impacts of Hurricanes on Coastal Communities

Beaches serve as a natural barrier between the ocean and inland communities, ecosystems, and natural resources. However, these dynamic environments move and change in response to winds, waves, and currents. During extreme storms, changes to beaches can be large, and the results are sometimes catastrophic. Lives may be lost, communities destroyed, and millions of dollars spent on rebuilding.

During storms, large waves may erode beaches, and high storm surge shifts the erosive force of the waves higher on the beach. In some cases, the combined effects of waves and surge may cause overwash or flooding. Building and infrastructure on or near a dune can be undermined during wave attack and subsequent erosion. During Hurricane Ivan in 2004, a five-story condominium in Orange Beach, Alabama, collapsed after the sand dune supporting the foundation eroded. The September 1999 landfall of Hurricane Dennis caused erosion and undermining that destroyed roads, foundations, and septic systems (fig. 1).

Figure 1. Parking areas, septic systems, and foundations in South Nags Head, North Carolina, collapsed when the underlying dune was eroded during the September 1999 landfall of Hurricane Dennis.

Waves overtopping a dune can transport sand inland, covering roads and blocking evacuation routes or emergency relief (fig. 2). If storm surge inundates barrier island dunes, currents flowing across the island can create a breach, or new inlet, completely severing evacuation routes. Waves and surge during the 2003 landfall of Hurricane Isabel left a 200-meter (m) wide breach that cut the only road to and from the village of Hatteras, N.C. (fig. 3).

Figure 2. Waves and surge left an overwash deposit covering roads during Hurricane Isabel in September 2003 (top). Parking areas near the beach and elevated homes (bottom) in Rodanthe, North Carolina, were filled during Hurricane Dennis in September 1999.

Extreme coastal changes caused by hurricanes may increase the vulnerability of communities both during a storm and to future storms. For example, when sand dunes on a barrier island are eroded substantially, inland structures are exposed to storm surge and waves. Absent or low dunes also allow water to flow inland across the island, potentially increasing storm surge in the back bay, on the soundside of the barrier, and on the mainland. During Hurricane Isabel the protective sand dunes near the breach were completely eroded, increasing vulnerability to future storms (fig. 4).

Figure 3. Storm surge, waves, and currents from Hurricane Isabel (August 2003) cut a breach across Highway 12 on Hatteras Island, North Carolina, severing the single road in and out of the village. The Atlantic Ocean is located to the left of the image. Asphalt from the highway is on the right side of the image. See figure 4 for aerial view of the breach.

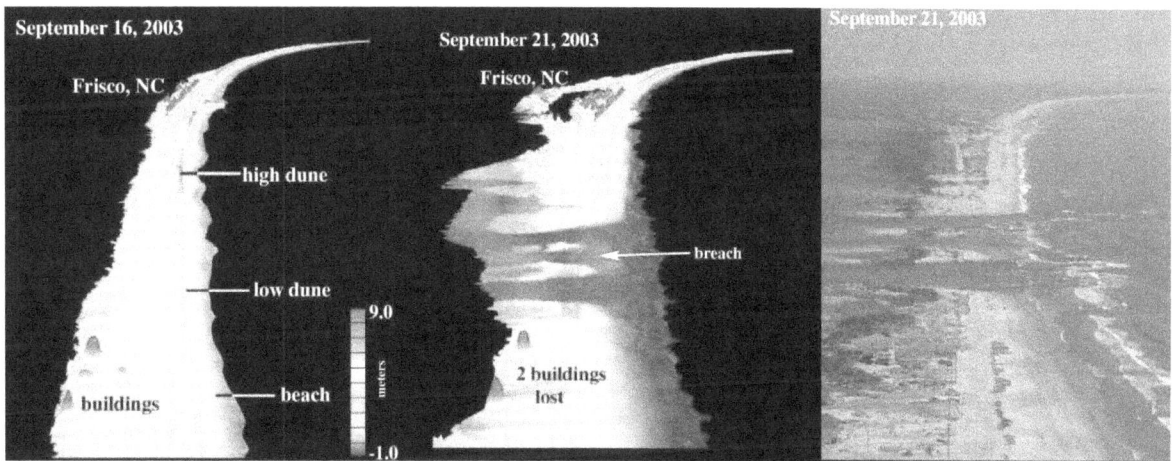

Figure 4. Lidar-based elevations of Hatteras Island, North Carolina, before (left) and after (middle) the landfall of Hurricane Isabel in September 2003 show erosion of the seaward-most dune and subsequent breaching (right). See figure 3 for a ground view of the breach. Note: Lidar surveys did not cover the same, or full, width of island during each survey.

1.2 Prediction of Hurricane-Induced Coastal Erosion

In the last decade, communities along the southeastern coast of the United States have been devastated by many powerful hurricanes including Isabel (2003), Frances (2004), Jeanne (2004), Irene (2011), and Sandy (2012). Waves and surge accompanying these storms resulted in widespread beach and dune erosion and extensive overwash (Sallenger and others, 2004, 2005, 2006; Morgan and Sallenger, 2009). A clear need exists to identify areas of our coastline that are likely to experience extreme erosion during a hurricane. This information can be used to determine vulnerability levels and the associated the risk of building houses or infrastructure on land that shifts and moves with each storm landfall. A decade of research on storm-driven coastal change hazards within the U.S. Geological Survey (USGS) National Assessment of Coastal Change Hazards project has provided the data and modeling capabilities to produce the first regional assessment of the vulnerability of coastlines to extreme erosion during hurricane landfall. Vulnerability is defined in terms of the probability for coastal change, predicted using a USGS-developed storm-impact scale that compares predicted elevations of hurricane-induced water levels to measured elevations of coastal topography (Sallenger, 2000). This approach defines four coastal change regimes that describe the dominant interactions between beach morphology and storm processes and resulting modes of coastal change. Here, the focus is on the vulnerability of open-coast sandy beaches on the U.S southeast Atlantic shoreline.

1.3 Storm-Scaling Model

During a storm, the combined effects of (1) the astronomical tide, (2) storm surge, and (3) wave runup (both setup, η_{setup}, and swash, S) move the erosive forces of the storm higher on the beach than during typical wave conditions. The total elevation of these three parameters defines two key metrics that characterize the nearshore hydrodynamic forcing of a storm: (1) the extreme high water level attained during a storm, defined here as the 98-percent exceedance level (η_{98}), and (2) the storm-induced mean water level (η_{50}), defined by only storm surge, tide, and wave setup.

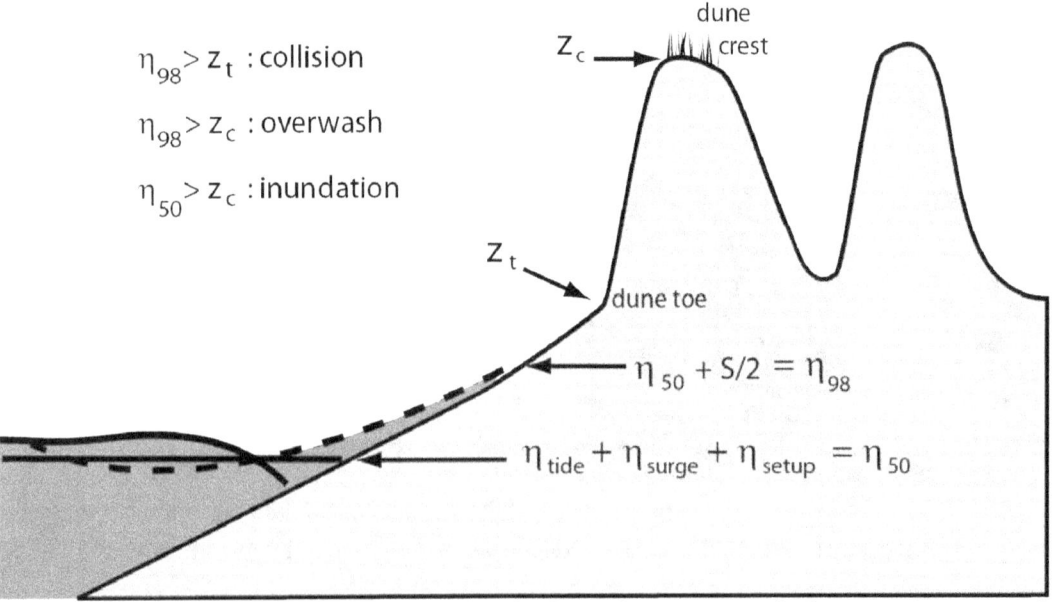

Figure 5.   Sketch defining the relevant morphologic and hydrodynamic parameters in the storm impact scaling model of Sallenger (2000) (modified from Stockdon and others, 2009).

Water-level elevations are compared to the elevation of the toe (z_t) and crest (z_c) of the most seaward sand dunes that define the landward limits of the beach system and represent the first-line defense of a barrier island to an approaching storm. Using these parameters, four storm-impact regimes, or thresholds for coastal change, are defined to provide a framework for examining the general types and relative magnitudes of coastal change that are likely to occur during hurricanes (fig. 5) (Sallenger, 2000; Stockdon and others, 2007a).

- *swash ($\eta_{98} < z_t$)*
- *collision ($\eta_{98} > z_t$)*
- *overwash ($\eta_{98} > z_c$)*
- *inundation ($\eta_{50} > z_c$)*

(Note: Following Plant and Stockdon (2012), our nomenclature differs from Sallenger (2000) to emphasize probabilistic definition of water levels and to clearly distinguish both the horizontal and vertical components of dune morphology.)

Collision	Overwash	Inundation

Figure 6.　Examples of post-storm conditions after collision (Nags Head, North Carolina; Isabel, 2003), overwash (Santa Rosa Island, Florida; Ivan, 2004), and inundation (Dauphin Island, Alabama; Katrina, 2005).

The *swash* regime represents a range of relatively calm weather conditions, where water levels are confined to areas seaward of the dune base. Sand that is eroded from the beach during more energetic periods is transported offshore and will return to the beach during more quiescent conditions. The erosion and recovery cycle can occur over a time span on the order of weeks. When waves reach the base of the dune (*collision* regime), the front of the dune is expected to erode (fig. 6, left). Again, sand is transported seaward and then re-deposited on the beach or sandbar or transported alongshore. In this case, the beach is likely to recover in the weeks and months following the storm. However, because aeolian processes are responsible for natural dune growth, recovery of the dune may take years.

In extreme cases, such as during stronger storms and for relatively lower dunes, waves and surge may exceed the dune crest elevation, resulting in *overwash*. Under these conditions, waves transport sand landward from the beach and dune (fig. 6, center). Impacts may be more long-lasting in this regime as sand is deposited inland, making it unavailable for natural recovery following a storm. During *inundation* of the beach (fig. 6, right), storm-induced mean water levels exceed the elevation of the crest of the primary dune or berm. Some of the most extreme coastal changes on barrier islands occur within this regime; the beach system (dune crest and beach) is completely submerged, and net landward transport of sediment is likely to occur (Sallenger, 2000). Typically, larger magnitudes of shoreline retreat and beach erosion will occur when the beach is inundated as a result of sand transport occurring under all storm scale regimes (Stockdon and others, 2007a). On narrow barrier islands, inundation allows strong currents to cross the island and focus where dunes are low, thus carving breaches.

The predictive accuracy of the storm-impact scaling model was tested by hindcasting the likely impacts of Hurricanes Bonnie (1998) and Floyd (1999) (Stockdon and others, 2007a) and of Hurricane Ivan (2004) (Stockdon and others, 2007b) and comparing these with observed morphologic changes. For Hurricane Ivan, the overall hindcast accuracy of the model in predicting one of the four regime types was 68 percent. The accuracy of the model varied among regimes and was highest for the overwash conditions. Underprediction of the actual storm response was more likely than overprediction. Errors were likely due to profile evolution of the low-lying barriers during the storm. As dune-crest elevation was lowered, the collision regime could proceed to overwash and then inundation.

With skillful hindcasting results, the model has also been applied in real time for landfalling hurricanes (Plant and others, 2010; see also *http://coastal.er.usgs.gov/hurricanes/sandy/coastal-change/*). Using pre-storm measurements of dune elevations and real-time forecasts of storm surge and wave conditions, the USGS routinely reports the likelihood of beaches experiencing coastal change associated with collision, overwash, and inundation. These analyses are posted online (*http://coastal.er.usgs.gov/hurricanes*) and revised with updated hydrodynamic forecasts as a storm approaches landfall.

Using a methodology similar to the real-time forecasts, this report quantifies the likely impact of hypothetical hurricane landfalls on the U.S. southeast Atlantic coastline. The probabilities of hurricane-induced coastal change are used to define the vulnerability of this region to extreme erosion from waves and storm surge associated with category 1–5 hurricanes. This report, along with a similar analysis for the Gulf of Mexico shorelines (Stockdon and others, 2012), forms the basis of a USGS national assessment of storm-induced coastal erosion hazards.

2. Methods

In order to use this model for a large-scale assessment of the potential for coastal change during future hurricane landfall, accurate estimates of (1) the dune parameters and (2) the expected hurricane-induced water level for hypothetical storms are needed. Well-documented models of storm surge have been used to estimate worst-case scenarios of water-level elevations for category 1–5 hurricanes and can be used directly by our modeling approach. Simulations of corresponding wave conditions for category 1–5 hurricane landfalls are more challenging, but given simplifying assumptions it is possible to determine worst-case scenario wave heights for each category. Numerical simulations of storm surge and wave heights support application of our approach to large stretches of coast. Light detection and ranging (lidar) topographic surveying has made it possible to accurately measure dune elevations along long (hundreds of kilometers) lengths of coastline. The combination of high-resolution measurements and advanced hydrodynamic modeling makes it possible to estimate probabilities of hurricane-induced coastal change and to identify coastal erosion vulnerability at a national scale.

2.1 Lidar-Derived Beach Morphology

The morphology of the beaches and dunes was mapped using airborne lidar topographic surveys conducted from 2009 to 2010 by the U.S. Army Corps of Engineers (USACE) Compact Hydrographic Airborne Rapid Total Survey (CHARTS) and the USGS Experimental Advanced Airborne Research Lidar (EAARL) systems. The combination of laser-based ranging with inertial and GPS-based navigation provides an efficient method for collecting high-resolution data of sub-aerial topography with sufficient accuracy (root-mean-square (RMS) vertical accuracy = 15 centimeters, cm; horizontal accuracy = 1 – 1.5 meters, m) to resolve the spatial details of sand-dune elevation and position (Sallenger and others, 2003). Three-dimensional lidar data were gridded using a fixed-scale interpolator (Plant and others, 2002), which allows for variability in cross-shore and alongshore resolution, here, 2.5 m and 10 m, respectively. In addition to a gridded topographic surface, this method produces a corresponding grid of the RMS error, which provides a measure of noise in the data. A Hanning filter with a width equal to two times the grid resolution was chosen to minimize noise in the data associated with vegetation, alongshore variability, and other error sources while preserving distinct morphology. Analysis of cross-shore profiles of gridded data allows for automated extraction of dune crest (z_c) and toe (z_t), as well as shoreline position (x_{sl}) and beach slope (β_m), at a regular alongshore interval, here, 10 m (fig. 7). These features are ultimately used to estimate wave runup and the corresponding storm-response regimes, as well as to measure actual morphologic changes before and after storms. Detailed descriptions of the algorithm used to extract shoreline position, dune crest and toe, and beach slope can be found in the first report of this series: National Assessment of Hurricane-Induced Coastal Erosion Hazards: Gulf of Mexico (Stockdon and others, 2012) and references contained therein.

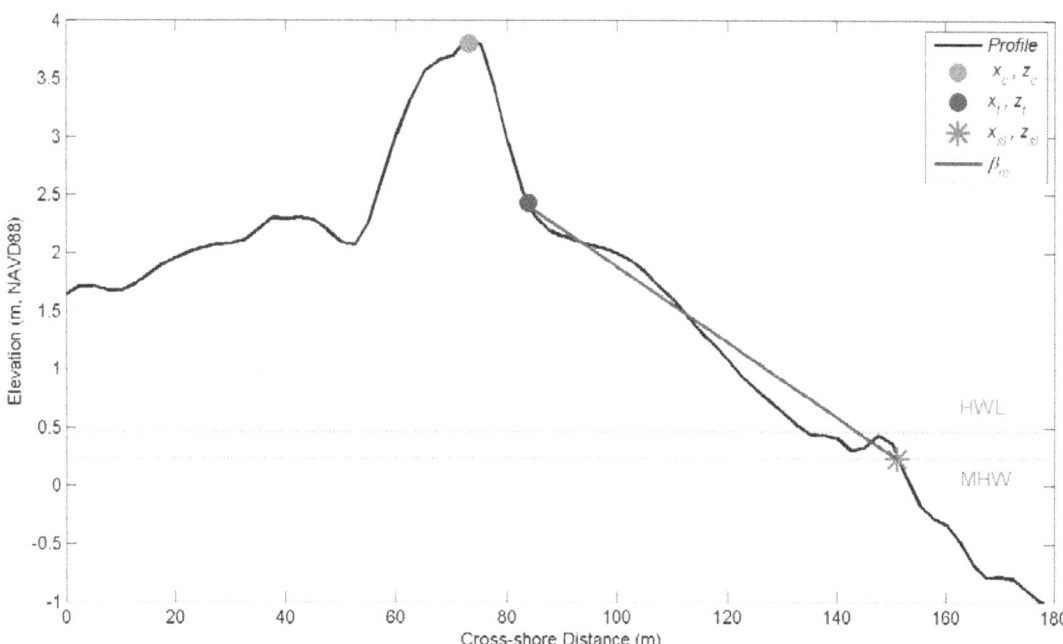

Figure 7. Cross-shore profile of gridded elevations indicating the locations of the dune crest (x_c, z_c), toe (x_t, z_t), shoreline (x_{sl}, z_{sl}), mean beach slope (β_m), mean high water (MHW), and high water line (HWL). Abbreviation: m, meter.

2.2 Hurricane-Induced Water Levels

During a hurricane, water levels at the shoreline include the combined effects of tide, storm surge, and local wave energy. Predictions of coastal change during hurricanes require estimates of both the mean and extreme water levels that can be expected for each category. The mean hurricane-induced water level, η_{50}, is defined as

$$\eta_{50} = \eta_{tide} + \eta_{surge} + \eta_{setup} \tag{1}$$

where η_{tide} is the astronomical tide level, η_{surge} is storm surge, and η_{setup} is wave setup, the super-elevation of the water surface at the shoreline due to wave breaking. The extreme water levels attained during the storm include wave swash, the time-varying component of wave energy on the beach, and are defined as

$$\eta_{98} = \eta_{50} + 1.1(S/2) \tag{2}$$

where S is the total swash excursion about the setup level and the 1.1 multiplier corrects for parameterization bias. It is important to note that both the mean and maximum water levels include a contribution from waves, which can increase water levels at the shoreline by the same magnitude as surge for category 1–3 hurricanes (Stockdon and others, 2007a).

2.2.1 Tide and Storm Surge

The predicted elevations of combined high tide and storm surge ($\eta_{tide} + \eta_{surge}$) for category 1–5 hurricanes were extracted from the National Oceanic and Atmospheric Administration (NOAA) SLOSH (Sea, Lake, and Overland Surges from Hurricanes) model, which has been used by NOAA in inundation risk studies and operational storm surge forecasting. The numerical model is based on linearized, depth-integrated equations of motion and continuity (Jarvinen and Lawrence, 1985). Storm surge is modeled by simulating the conditions of each category storm approaching the coast from different angles and at varying speeds. Changes in maximum surge elevations are forced by time-varying wind-stress and pressure-gradients that depend on the hurricane location, minimum pressure, and the radius of maximum winds (Jarvinen and Lawrence, 1985).

Storm surge levels ($\eta_{tide} + \eta_{surge}$) are simulated for each storm category in each of 10 model domains subdividing the southeast Atlantic region. These simulations represent the peak water levels in each domain forced by thousands of hypothetical storms of varying forward speed, size, and direction, under mean-higher-high water tide conditions. The maximum surge within each grid cell, or the maximum of the maximum (MOM), represents a worst-case, localized surge level that could occur for a nearby hurricane landfall (fig. 8). (Note that the MOM is a composite from many storms and does not represent water levels that would occur along the entire coast for a single storm.) The resulting spatial variations in maximum storm surge reflect local water depths, proximity to bays and rivers, and so on and are accurate to ±20 percent of the calculated value (NOAA, 2007). Prediction errors in the SLOSH model can arise from differences between the parametric wind models, which force SLOSH, and the actual hurricane wind field (Houston and others, 1999) as well as discrepancies between the coarse model grid and the actual topography and bathymetry over which the storm will travel. Additional constraints were applied to address some practical implementation problems associated with our use of the MOMs and are described in detail in Stockdon and others (2012).

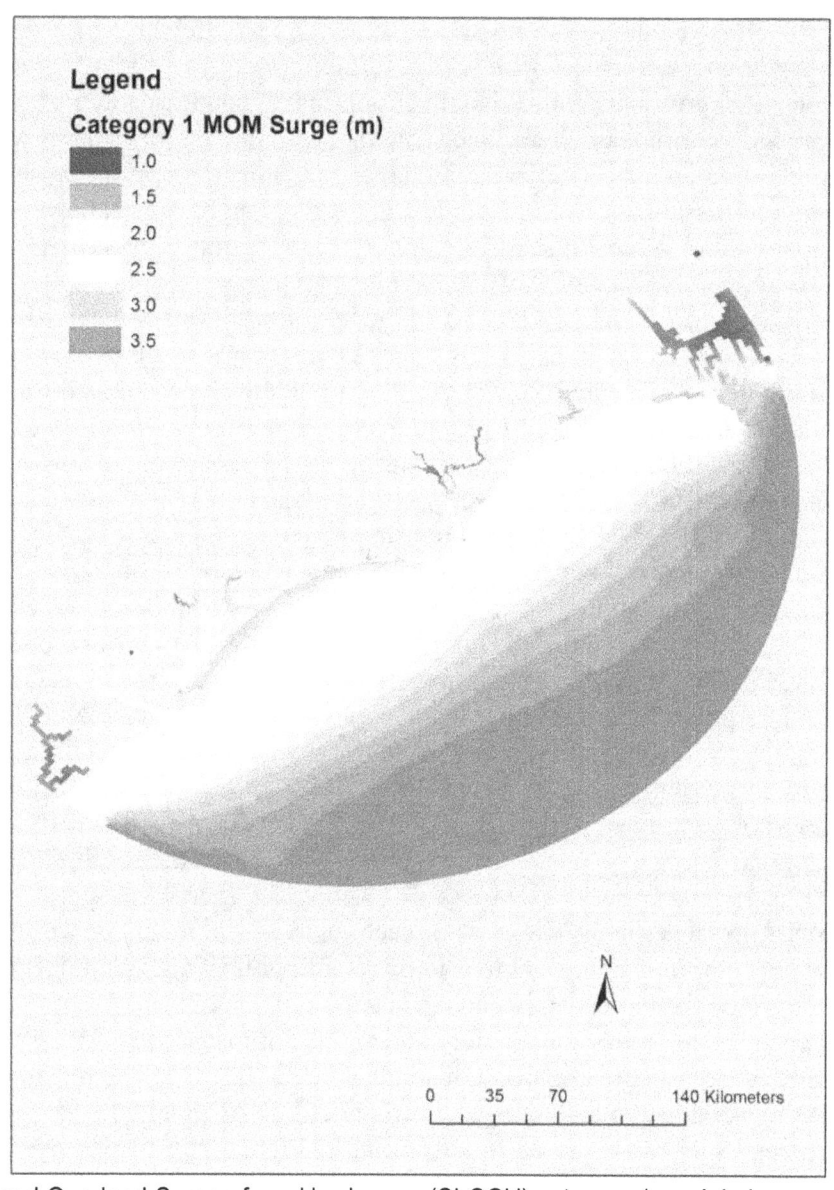

Legend

Category 1 MOM Surge (m)

- 1.0
- 1.5
- 2.0
- 2.5
- 3.0
- 3.5

N

0 35 70 140 Kilometers

Figure 8. Sea, Lake, and Overland Surges from Hurricanes (SLOSH) category 1 modeled surge maximum of the maximum (MOM) for the Wilmington/Myrtle Beach basin. Abbreviation: m, meter.

2.2.2. Wave Height and Period

Wave conditions vary spatially and temporally during hurricanes due to the same factors that cause variation in storm surge. Unfortunately, there is no equivalent of the MOMs that can be used to specify maximum wave height and period for category 1–5 hurricanes. Observations during hurricanes are incomplete as instrumented buoys tend to fail during conditions stronger than tropical storm. Long-term hindcasts of historical wave conditions (for example, USACE Wave Information Studies [WIS]) also underrepresent storm conditions. Therefore, wave conditions were estimated using the Simulating WAves Nearshore (SWAN) model, a spectral wave model that resolves random, short-crested, wind-generated waves varying in time and space (Holthuijsen and others, 1993).

One approach to calculating storm-wave parameters would be to simulate individual idealized hurricanes in SWAN, much like was done with SLOSH in order to build a MOM-consistent dataset. However, an attempt to cover the entire coastline with idealized hurricane tracks, and include a sufficient sampling of storm parameter space (wind speed, radius of maximum winds, forward speed, and so on), would require a massive computational effort. Furthermore, because we require wave information at a specific shallow water depth (20 m), the height of hurricane waves will tend to be limited by dissipation due to breaking, white-capping, and friction. Consequently, the sensitivity of parameterized shoreline water levels to wave parameter errors is expected to be limited as well.

Therefore, we apply a simple approach of generating stationary waves (in time) using SWAN for the maximum wind speed that defines each hurricane category over the entire southeast Atlantic basin. For determination of the contribution of waves to the total hurricane-induced water levels, the maximum wave-height value from an ensemble of simulations of the maximum wind speed was selected as the representative value for each category, very similar to the MOM product from the SLOSH model. As with the MOMs, these results do not represent an individual storm but rather a composite worst-case estimate at each location from many storm scenarios.

For our analysis, SWAN version 40.85 was used. The model was run in third-generation mode using the Westhuysen formulation for white-capping and Yan formulation for wind input (GEN3 WESTH). Bottom friction was included using default values, and all other model parameters were left as default. The resolution of the SWAN computational grid was 2 kilometers (km) x 2 km (fig. 9). Bathymetry was interpolated from the National Geophysical Data Center (NGDC) Coastal Relief Model (CRM). The Cape Hatteras Inundation digital elevation model (DEM) was used to fill a gap in the CRM off Cape Hatteras at the shelf break. A nested 100 m x 500 m (cross-shore x alongshore) rectangular grid for south Florida was nested in the larger domain. This was needed to resolve the 20 m isobath, where significant wave height (H_s) is extracted for analysis, along the south Florida coast where the continental shelf is very narrow. SWAN was run 24 times for each wind speed with direction varying from 15° to 360° at 15° increments (fig. 9). For each wind speed, the model results from the 24 wind direction runs were combined into a single grid by retaining the wave parameters from the wind direction that generated the largest H_s in each grid cell.

Simulated H_s at the 20-m isobaths for category 1–5 hurricanes was relatively uniform along the southeast Atlantic coast with the exception of south Florida (fig. 10). The resulting maximum wave heights at the 20-m isobaths typically ranged from about 7 m to about 9 m, except in south Florida, where the continental shelf was very narrow resulting in higher maximum wave height values. To put these model results in context, we compared the modeled wave heights to observed wave heights at several buoys located in different water depths throughout the southeast Atlantic. Maximum observed wave heights were between 5 m and 10 m at relatively shallow locations (that is, 15 to 30 m water depths, which included just three buoys). The simulated wave heights are representative of maximum possible wave heights for each hurricane category.

The swash parameterization requires estimates of peak period, which were not reliably estimated due to our simplified wind field. Consistent peak-period estimates were obtained from an analysis of 20 years of NOAA National Data Buoy Center data for 28 shallow-water buoys (< 30 m) operating in the southeast Atlantic. The analysis yielded a parameterized relation between significant wave height, obtained from the SWAN model, and peak wave periods (fig. 11).

$$T_p = b_0 + b_1 * H_s + b_2 * H_s^2 + b_3 h, \tag{3}$$

where Tp is peak wave period, H_s is significant wave height, and h is the depth corresponding to each wave period and height. Data from all buoys in water depths less than 30 m were used in a linear regression to estimate the model coefficients, b_n, resulting in

$$b_0 = 7.3111 \ (\pm 0.0374)$$
$$b_1 = 0.4367 \ (\pm 0.0225)$$
$$b_2 = 0.0677 \ (\pm 0.0037)$$
$$b_3 = -0.0136 \ (\pm 0.0015)$$

This parameterization was used to compute peak wave periods for each hurricane category that were consistent with southeast Atlantic observations, using the simulated significant wave heights and the 20-m depth as input.

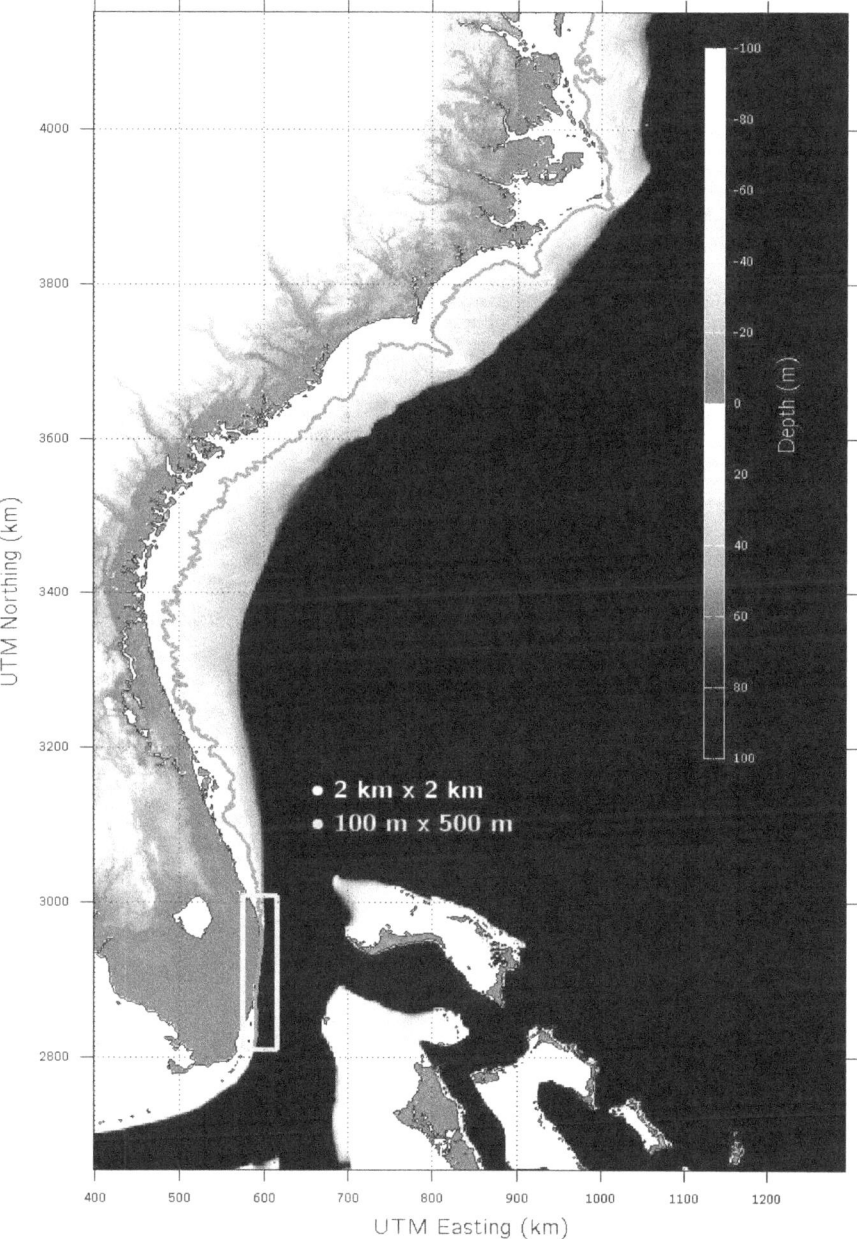

Figure 9. Simulating WAves Nearshore (SWAN) model computational grid. Longitudinal and latitudinal resolution is 2 kilometers. The green box represents a finer (100 m x 500 m) nested grid designed to resolve the narrow continental shelf in southeast Florida. The 20-meter isobath along the U.S. coastline is shown in red. Abbreviation: m, meter.

11

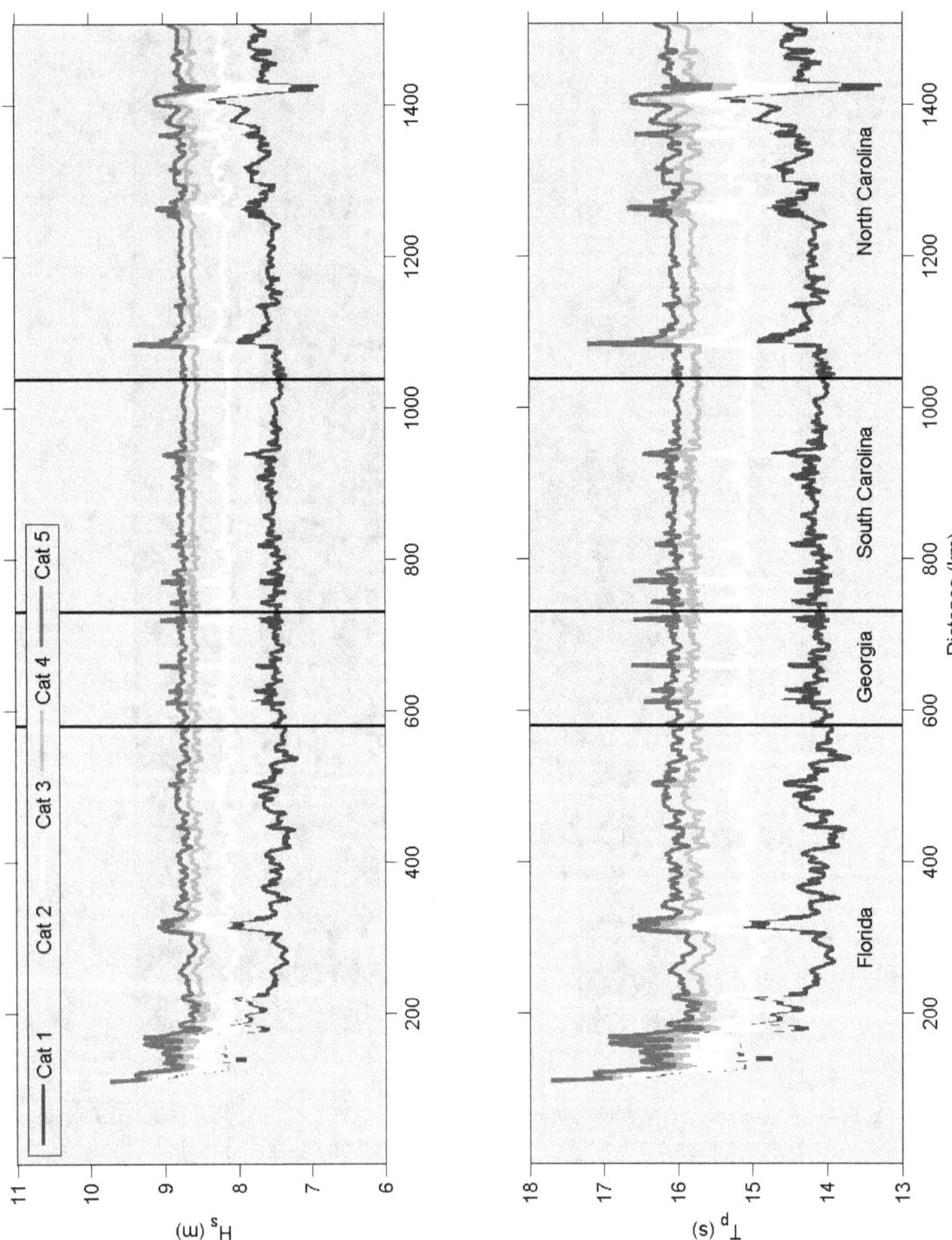

Figure 10. Modeled significant wave height (H_s, top) and parameterized peak period (T_p, bottom) at the 20-meter isobath extending from Florida (left) to North Carolina (right). State boundaries are indicated by vertical lines. Abbreviations: m, meter; km, kilometer; s, second.

12

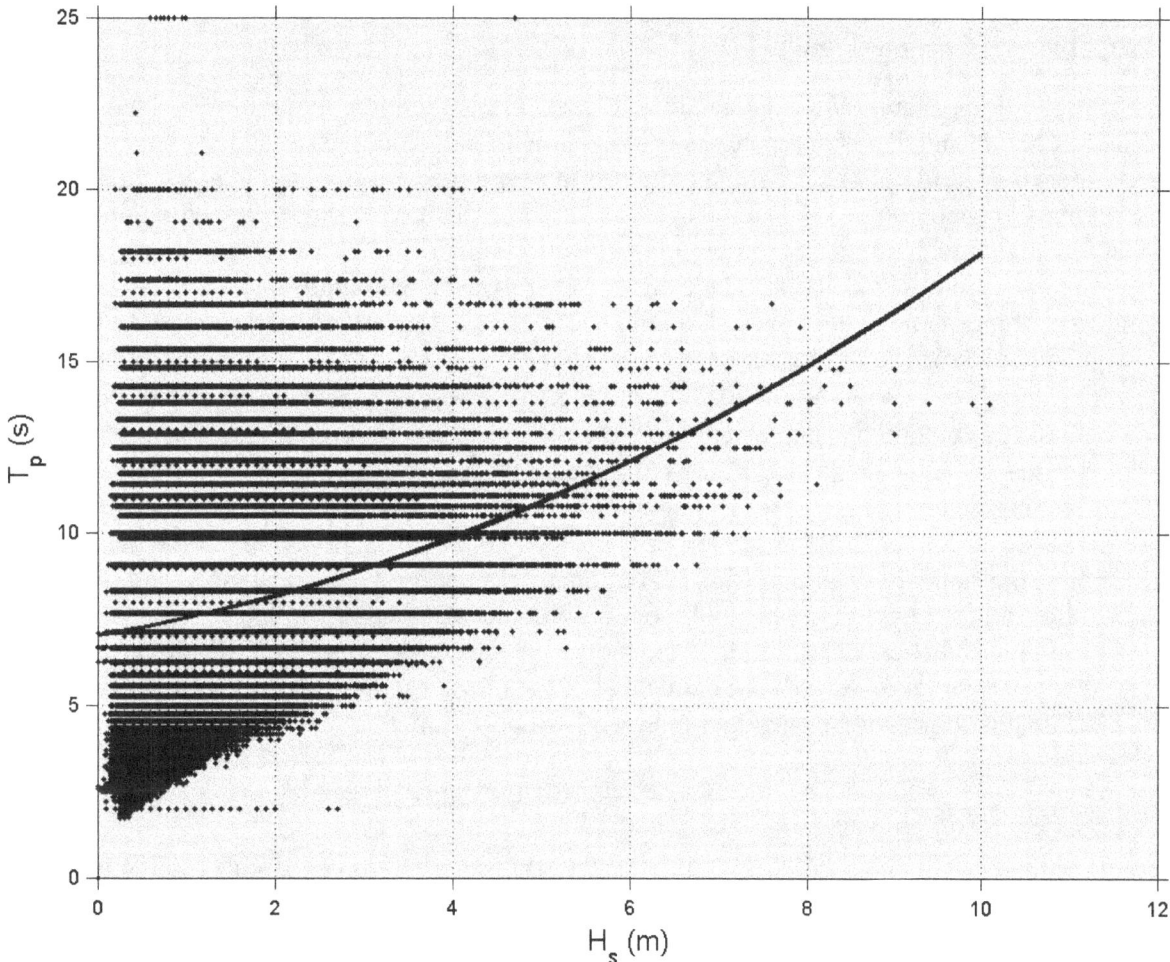

Figure 11. Significant wave height (H_s) and peak (T_p) wave periods for shallow (h < 30 m) water observed at National Data Buoy Center buoys. The black curve represents the weighted regression based on shallow water buoys. Abbreviations: m, meter; s, second.

2.2.3 Wave Setup and Swash

Swash and setup, the wave-induced components of total shoreline water levels, are parameterized using modeled wave conditions and measured beach slope (Stockdon and others, 2006). Setup, required in calculation of both mean (η_{50}) and extreme (η_{98}) hurricane-induced water levels, is parameterized as

$$\eta_{setup} = 0.35\beta_m \left(H_0 L_0\right)^{1/2} \tag{4}$$

where $L_0 = gT_p^2/2\pi$. Wave swash, S, the time-varying component of water levels at the shoreline and part of the calculation of extreme (η_{98}) hurricane-induced water levels, is parameterized as

$$S = \left[H_0 L_0 \left(0.563\beta_m^2 + 0.005\right)\right]^{1/2} \tag{5}$$

13

Combining equations (4) and (5) with modeled η_{tide} and η_{surge} provided estimates of hurricane-induced mean and maximum water levels (equations 1 and 2).

2.3 Probability of Coastal Change

Probabilities of coastal change are based on estimating the likelihood that the beach system will experience erosion and deposition patterns consistent with collision, overwash, or inundation regimes. Uncertainties that were incorporated in the probability estimates arise from that associated with measurements of topographic elevation (for example, lidar positional and interpolation uncertainties) and that associated with predicting wave runup elevations.

The probabilities of collision (dune erosion), overwash, and inundation were calculated using distributions of morphologic and hydrodynamic parameters extracted from 1-km sections of coast. Hydrodynamic and morphologic data were co-located alongshore using a common reference line (the 20-yr high water line (HWL) shoreline). Morphologic features, z_c, z_t, and β_m, were interpolated to the reference line and smoothed using a Hanning window with a full width of 2 km. Each interpolated, smoothed value of (x_c, z_c), (x_t, z_t), and β_m was assigned a RMS error calculated from the scatter of the data in the smoothing window (fig. 12, top). The variables were represented with a normal distribution of values at the location of each 1-km section of coast using the interpolated value as the mean and the RMS error as the standard deviation (fig. 12, bottom). This analysis produced mean and standard deviations for both the hydrodynamic and the morphologic variables.

Using the statistical distribution of the input values at each alongshore location, the probability, p, that the total water level exceeds the dune crest or toe elevation threshold for a particular storm regime is calculated from the normal cumulative distribution function

$$p = \frac{1}{\sigma\sqrt{2\pi}} \int_0^\infty e^{\frac{-(t-\mu)^2}{2\sigma^2}} \, dt \tag{6}$$

where μ is the mean difference between either the mean (inundation) or extreme (collision, overwash) water levels and either the dune toe (collision) or dune crest (overwash, inundation) regime. The variance of the difference, σ^2, is the sum of the variances of the inputs. Thus, the probabilities of each storm-impact regime are calculated as:

- collision: $p_c = probability\ ([\,\eta_{98} - z_t] > 0)$
- overwash: $p_o = probability\ ([\,\eta_{98} - z_c] > 0)$
- inundation: $p_i = probability\ ([\,\eta_{50} - z_c] > 0)$

For example, figure 12 shows the cumulative distribution of $(\eta_{98} - x_c)$ for a 1-km section of coast for a category 1 hurricane. The probability that this value exceeds zero defines the likelihood that overwash will occur at this location.

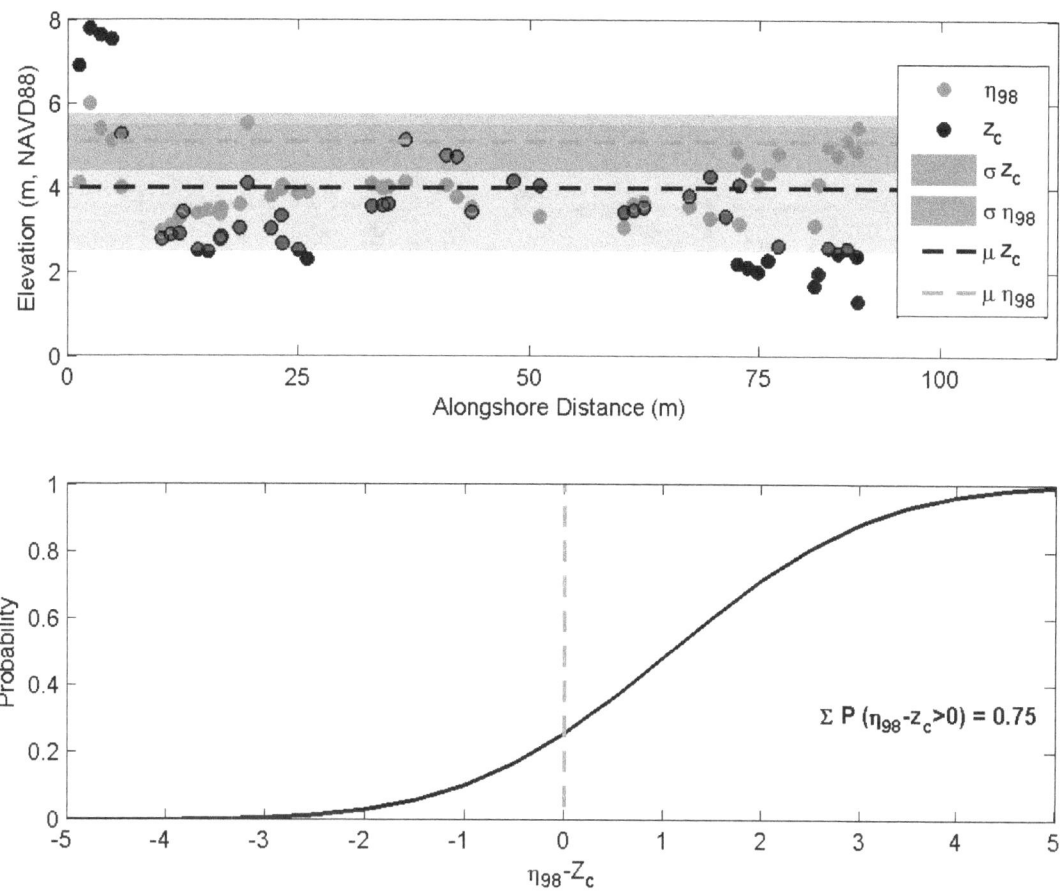

Figure 12.   Maximum shoreline water level (η_{98}) for a category 1 hurricane and raw and smoothed dune crest elevation (z_c) for a 1-kilometer alongshore section (top). Shaded areas indicate the RMS error about the mean value within the section. Cumulative probability distribution, $p(\eta_{98}\text{-}z_c)$ where the sum of p over the range ($\eta_{98}\text{-}z_c$)>0 defines the probability of overwash (bottom). Abbreviation: m, meter.

3. Results

3.1 Coastal Morphology

Dune morphologies along the southeast Atlantic coast vary extensively over both short and long spatial scales (table 1). Mean dune crest elevation, μz_c, for sandy beaches in this region is 3.84 m, and the standard deviation, σ, is 1.40 m, indicating spatial variability high enough that low elevations ($\mu - 2\sigma$) are just above the HWL (fig. 13, top). Elevations range from 1 to 10 m. Dune toe elevations are consistently low with less spatial variability (fig. 14, middle; $\mu z_t = 2.26$ m; $\sigma z_c = 0.69$ m).   Local spatial variability tends to scale with dune elevation; locations with higher mean elevations often exhibit greater spatial variability (fig. 14).

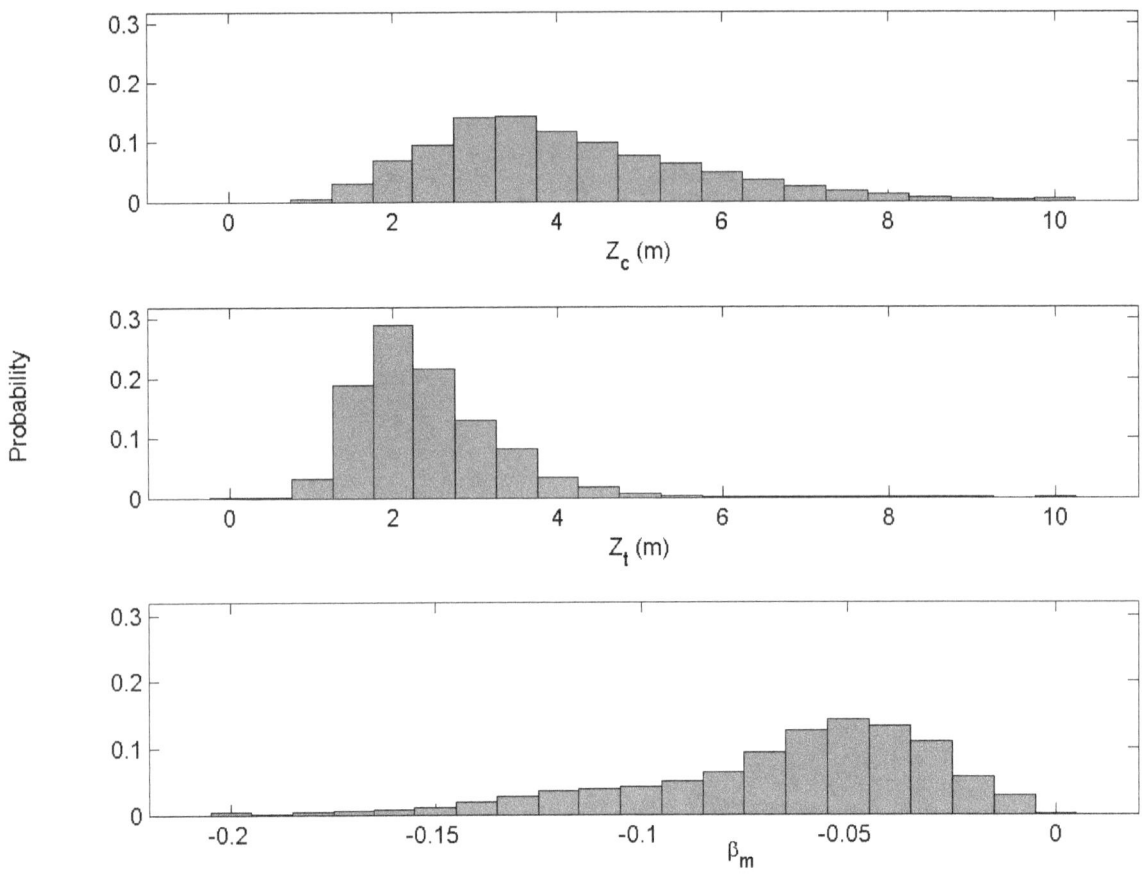

Figure 13. Distributions of dune crest elevation (z_c, top), dune toe elevation (z_t, middle), and mean beach slope (β_m, bottom) for the southeast Atlantic sandy coastlines. Abbreviation: m, meter.

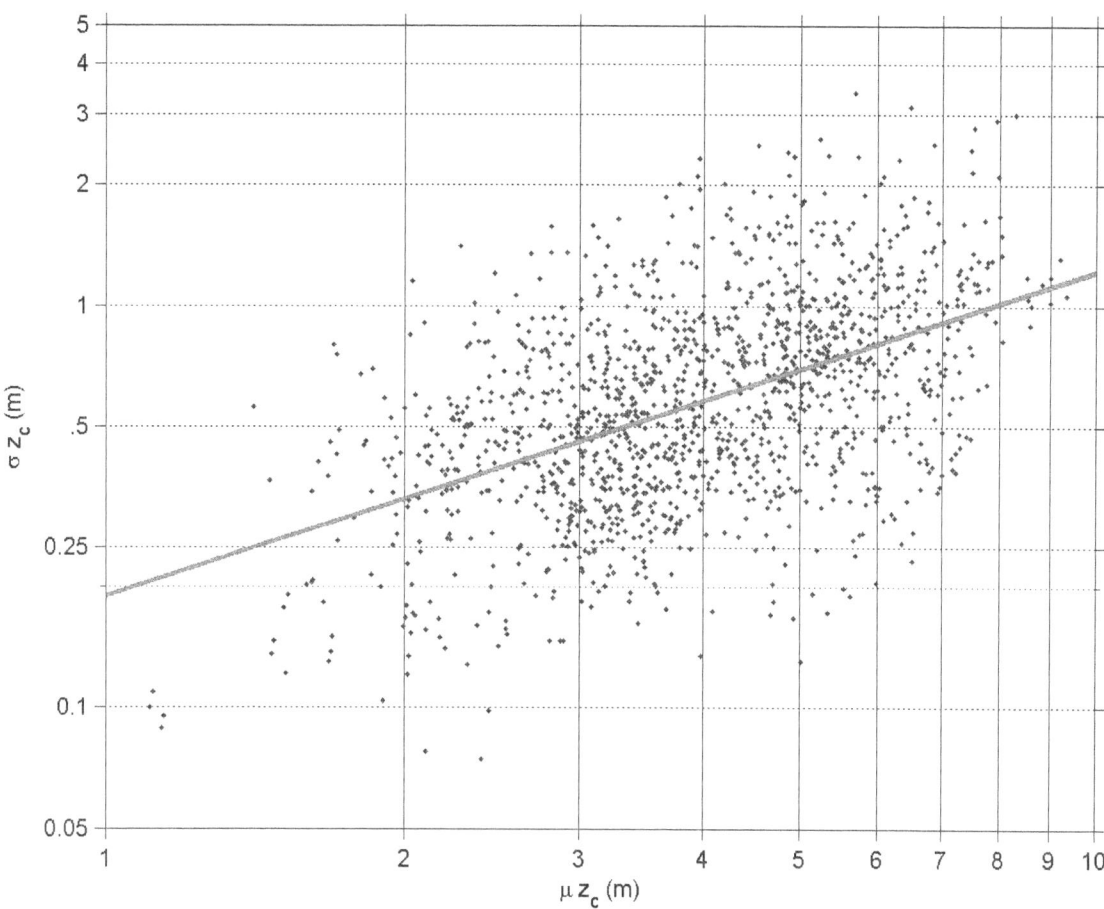

Figure 14. Mean dune crest elevation (μz_c) for 1-kilometer sections of coastline compared to the standard deviation (σz_c) in those sections. The red line indicated the best fit line between the two variables. $r^2 = 0.25$, N = 1455. Note data are plotted on a log-log scale. Abbreviation: m, meter.

The highest dunes (z_c in excess of 9 m) are located in north Florida and northern North Carolina (figs. 15–16); however, variability is high in both states, as noted by σz_c of 1.52 m ($\mu z_c = 4.71$ m) and 1.73 m ($\mu z_c = 4.44$ m), respectively. The lowest elevations are found along the coast of South Carolina ($\mu z_c = 2.93$ m; $\sigma z_c = 0.85$ m) and northern Georgia (μz_c 3.28 m; $\sigma z_c = 1.50$ m).

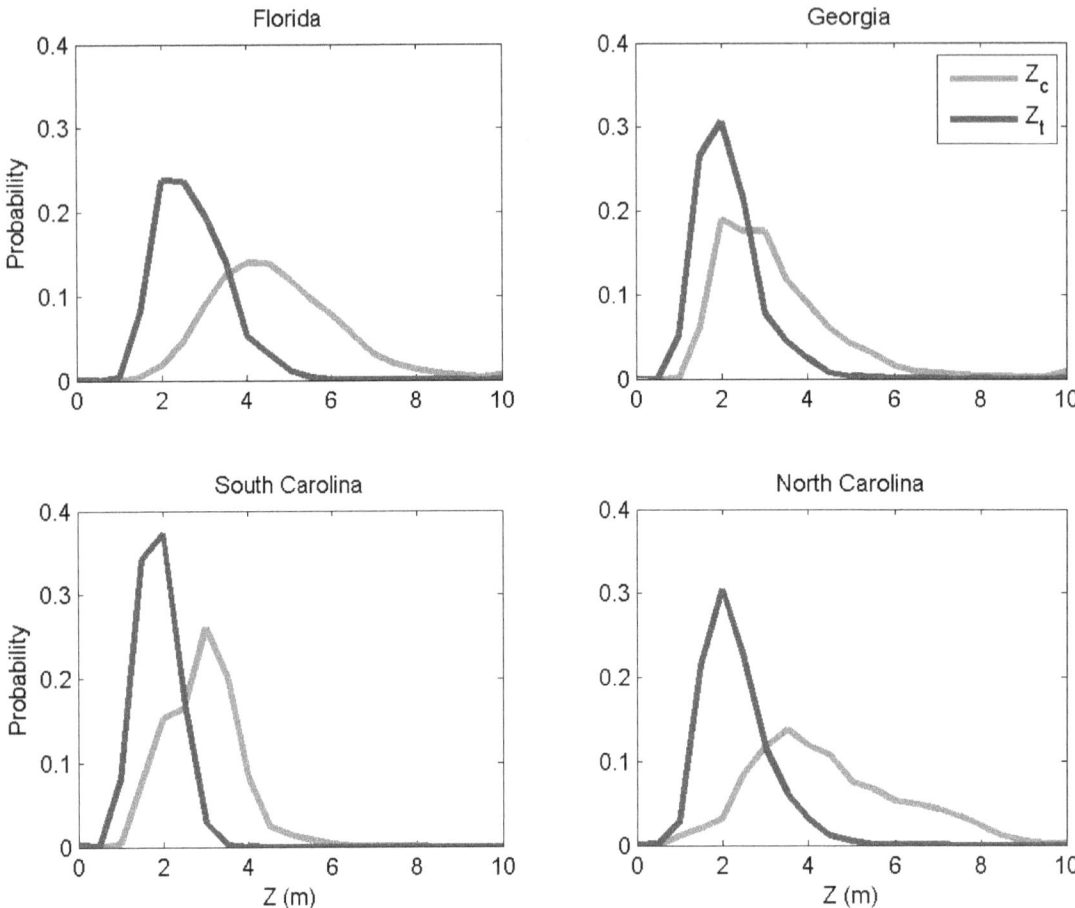

Figure 15. Distribution of dune crest (z_c) and dune toe (z_t) elevations for Florida, Georgia, South Carolina, and North Carolina. Abbreviation: m, meter.

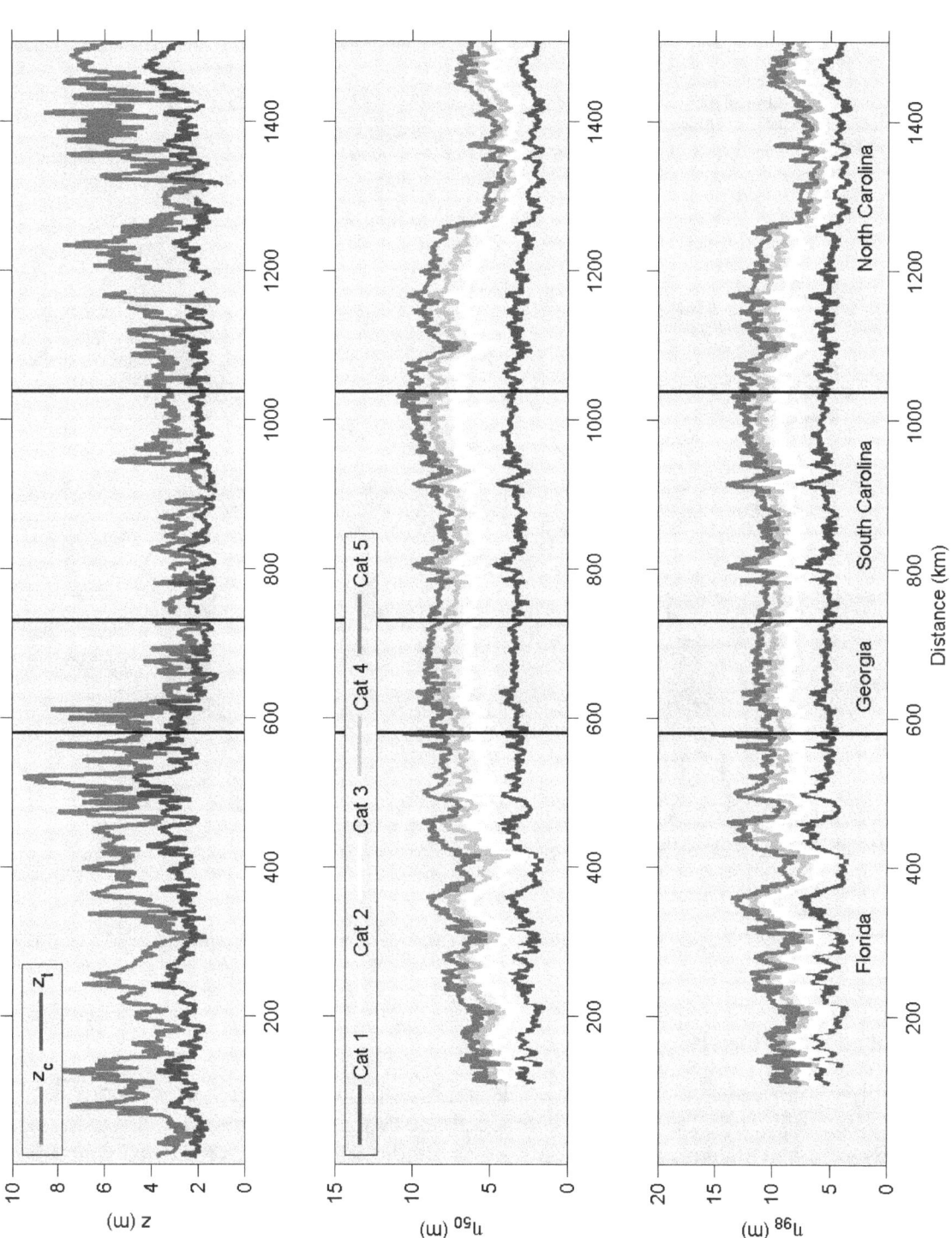

Figure 16. Dune crest (z_c) and toe (z_t) elevations (top) and hurricane-induced mean (η_{50}; middle) and maximum (η_{98}; bottom) shoreline water levels extending from Florida (left) to North Carolina (right). State boundaries are indicated by vertical lines. Abbreviation: m, meter; km, kilometer.

Although also spatially variable, mean beach slope is generally low (fig. 17), leading to dissipative conditions during storms. The lowest slopes, and least spatial variability, are located along the Georgia coast ($\mu\beta = 0.041$; $\sigma\beta = 0.019$). Steeper slopes are present along the Florida coast ($\mu\beta = 0.082$); however, the standard deviation was also greatest along the Florida coast ($\sigma\beta = 0.041$).

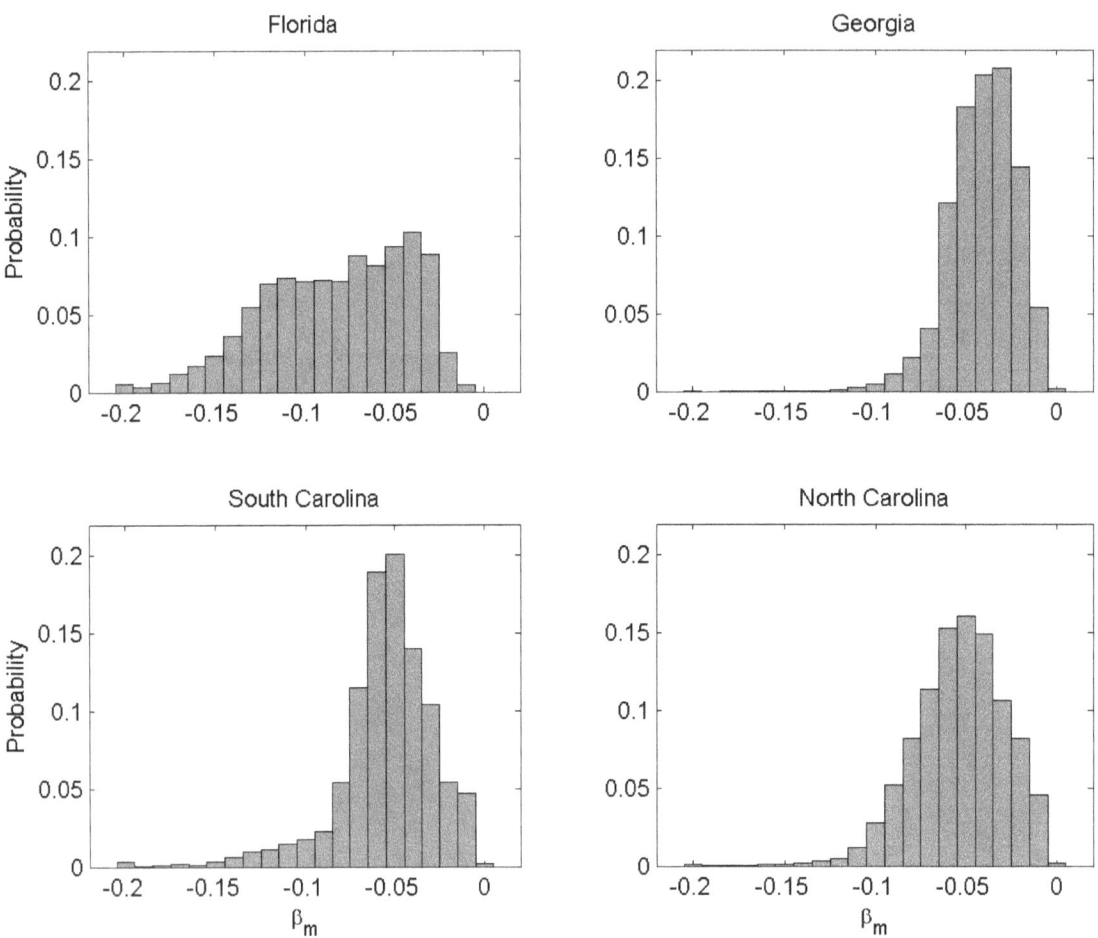

Figure 17. Distributions of mean beach slope (β_m) elevations for Florida, Georgia, South Carolina, and North Carolina.

3.2 Hurricane-Induced Water Levels

The variability of hurricane-induced water levels can be attributed to both hydrodynamics and beach morphology. Variability of H_s at $h = 20$ m within a single category, due to local bathymetry and dissipation from depth-limited breaking, white-capping, and bottom friction, leads to corresponding alongshore differences in η_{98} and η_{50}. The largest waves were located offshore of south Florida where a narrow shelf allows larger waves to make it to the nearshore (fig. 10), as wave breaking and, to a lesser extent, bottom dissipation act over very short distances before reaching the 20-m isobath. However, for the sandy beaches used in this analysis, variability of H_s along the shoreline for a single category is minimal; standard deviation of H_s ranges from 28 cm for a category 1 storm to 11 cm for a category 5 storm (table 2).

Smaller scale spatial variability of η_{98} is dominated by alongshore variations in β_m (fig. 17), as the wave-driven components of shoreline water levels, η_{setup} and S, are dependent on both input wave conditions and local slopes (equations 4 and 5). For similar input wave conditions, steeper beach slopes result in higher total runup elevations ($\eta_{R2} = 1.1[\eta_{setup} + S/2]$). For example, modeled category 3 wave heights were 8.2 m for both Florida and Georgia coastlines. However, η_{R2} is a meter higher on the Florida coast than in Georgia because of the steeper slopes: $\beta_m = 0.082$ in Florida as opposed to $\beta_m = 0.041$ in Georgia.

The modeling exercise demonstrated the relative importance of waves with respect to storm surge. For a category 1 storm, wave-driven components represent 63 percent of the total hurricane-induced water levels; the remaining 27 percent is attributed to tides and surge (table 2). For a category 2 storm, the contributions are approximately equal, 53 percent from waves and 47 percent from combined tides and surge. In a category 5 hurricane, surge dominates the signal, contributing 61 percent to the total water-level elevation. Wave height does not grow as rapidly due to dissipation through white-capping and breaking; however, surge continues to grow, approximately 1 m with each category.

3.3 Probability of Coastal Change

The probabilities of collision, overwash, and inundation indicate whether a specified coastal change regime is very likely (probability >90 percent), likely (>66 percent), about as likely as not (33 to 66 percent), unlikely (<33 percent), and very unlikely (<10 percent) given the local landfall of each hypothetical storm scenario. (Range descriptions are based on guidance from the Intergovernmental Panel on Climate Change (IPCC) (Le Treut and others, 2007).) Probabilities of coastal change for the lowest category hurricane show the vulnerability of beaches along the southeast Atlantic coast to dune erosion and overwash (fig. 18). For direct landfall of the lowest category hurricane, 89 percent of sandy beaches are very likely to experience dune erosion due to collision and nearly half (47 percent) of the coastal areas are vulnerable to overwash (table 3). Inundation of the beach and dune system is expected along 12 percent of the coastline, typically near areas with low elevation beach berms (the Georgia and South Carolina coasts, fig. 18). For a category 5 hurricane landfall, 92 percent of southeast Atlantic beaches are very likely to experience overwash and associated beach and dune erosion (table 3), and the percentage of beaches that are very likely to be inundated increases to 75 percent.

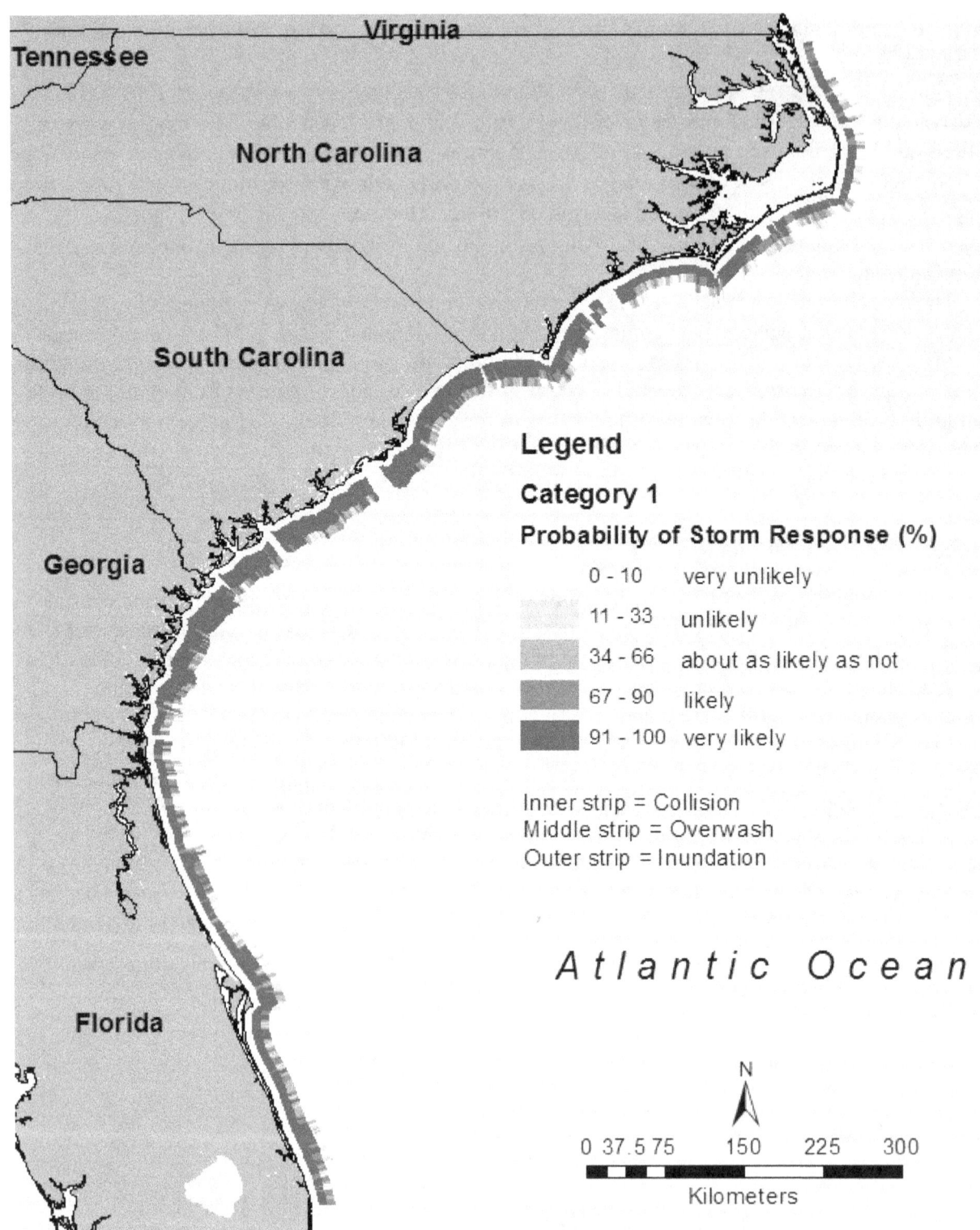

Figure 18. Probabilities of collision (inner strip), overwash (middle strip), and inundation (outer strip) during a category 1 hurricane for Florida, Georgia, South Carolina, and North Carolina.

Spatial variability exists over smaller spatial scales on the order of kilometers in areas with complex dune fields or extensive three-dimensional beach morphology. For example, in north Florida, the mix of low and high dunes leads to a more complicated picture of hurricane-induced erosion hazards (fig. 18). The smaller scale variability (alongshore spacing of 1 km) for a specific area can be examined using interactive maps that are available online. The probability of each mode of coastal change for category 1–5 landfalls, as well as supporting morphology and water level data, are available online (*http://coastal.er.usgs.gov/hurricanes/erosionhazards/*).

4. Discussion

4.1 Validity of Assumptions

This analysis is based on an estimate of a worst-case scenario with respect to storm surge levels and wave heights associated with each hurricane category. The implied assumption is that each location along the coast experiences the right-front quadrant of the hurricane at landfall, which results in onshore-directed winds and the combined effects of both the circulation and the forward motion of the storm.

Waves and surge associated with an actual storm may be significantly different than model results. The SLOSH results are grouped by Saffir-Simpson categories, which are based on wind speeds. It is recognized that wind-based Saffir-Simpson categories are not always an accurate indicator of expected storm surge (Irish and others, 2008, 2009); however, they do provide a convenient way to represent the data based on storm intensity, allowing users to examine a range of conditions in a small number of scenarios. Real-time analysis of individual landfalling hurricanes includes more realistic updates of surge, tides, and waves (*http://coastal.er.usgs.gov/hurricanes/*).

This assessment also assumes that the existing lidar-surveyed topography is up to date and accurately and synchronously reflects dune and beach morphology. Significant changes to beach and dune morphology between the survey date and dates of future hurricane landfall may affect the probabilities of coastal change. We assume that dune elevations change relatively slowly under non-storm conditions. Changes in beach slope, which will in turn affect the elevation of wave runup, may occur more frequently, as the foreshore profile adjusts to the daily wave climate. However, use of a mean beach slope (fig. 7) in this analysis provides a more temporally stable estimate of slope and hence a more consistent measure of storm-induced wave runup.

4.2 Relative Importance of Waves and Storm Surge

Hurricane-induced coastal changes are caused by waves and surge and the interaction of these processes with coastal morphology. Waves (setup and swash) were shown to increase water levels at the shoreline by 170 percent for a category 1 storm when compared to considering storm surge alone. Using a regional average of wave height and period for a category 1 hurricane (table 2), the predicted wave-driven component of shoreline water levels, η_{R2}, was 3.26 m, high enough to reach the mean dune toe elevation ($z_t = 2.36$ m), even without surge. For the category 2 conditions modeled in this analysis, the wave-driven and storm surge components were of similar magnitudes (3.42 m and 3.05 m, respectively). During a category 5 storm, the magnitude of surge was almost one and a half times that of the wave component; however, the magnitude of runup was 4 m, exceeding the mean dune crest height (3.84 m; table 1). This indicates that the waves alone are large enough make dunes in this area vulnerable to extreme erosion.

4.3 Assessment Updates

The vulnerability of sandy beaches can be expected to change in the future due to variations in storminess, sea-level rise, and human engineering efforts that alter beach configurations. As new observations and storm predictions become available, assessments may be revised to provide updated probabilities as well as a synthesis of how coastal vulnerability to storms changes in the future (*http://coastal.er.usgs.gov/hurricanes/erosionhazards/*). Specifically, coastal topography will be updated to account for actual storm-driven, or even engineered, changes to the coast associated with hurricane recovery, coastal restoration, and mitigation. This updating process is underway nearly continuously as USGS, U.S. Army Corps of Engineers, State agencies, and other entities utilize increasingly effective lidar capabilities in acquiring coastal coverage for a variety of surveying needs. Examples of these updates associated with major hurricane landfall can be found at *http://coastal.er.usgs.gov/hurricanes/*. In addition, as modeling capabilities advance, such as improvements to include storm size (Irish and others, 2008), surge inputs to coastal change analyses can be updated accordingly.

5. Conclusion

This assessment quantifies the probabilities of dune erosion, dune overwash, and beach/dune inundation during the landfall of category 1–5 hurricanes. The probabilities were calculated by comparing beach/dune elevations to modeled estimates of the hurricane-induced total water level at the shoreline, including contributions from both waves and storm surge. The beaches, coastal infrastructure, and habitat of the southeast Atlantic coast are vulnerable to extreme coastal changes during landfall of even category 1 hurricanes. The severity of these changes increases as the intensity of the storm-driven surge and waves increases and as the height of protective dunes decreases. Citizens and coastal managers who need to understand, plan for, and adapt to different levels of vulnerability will benefit from guidance on the likelihood of encountering mild, moderate, or severe erosion and deposition (overwash) associated with different storm intensities.

By including wave-driven setup and swash in addition to storm surge, we have identified the relative importance of waves in terms of their impact on erosion vulnerability. For category 1 to 2 hurricanes in this region, modeled wave runup is of greater magnitude than storm surge. As storm intensity increases, the relative importance of storm surge grows at a fast rate as nearshore wave height is limited due to dissipation by white-capping and breaking. Analyses that ignore the wave component of this problem will underestimate erosion vulnerability, particularly for lower category storms (or even weak tropical storms or cold fronts) .

The combination of large waves and surges in a region with low coastal elevations makes the entire southeast Atlantic vulnerable to significant coastal erosion during storms. In the direct landfall of a category 1 hurricane, 89 percent of dune-backed beaches along the southeast Atlantic coast are very likely (*p*>90 percent) to experience dune erosion during the collision regime. Overwash during a category 1 landfall is very likely along 47 percent of the coast. During category 5 conditions, 92 percent of the southeast Atlantic beaches are very likely to experience overwash and associated erosion, and 75 percent of the beaches and dunes are very likely to be vulnerable to erosion due to inundation.

6. Acknowledgments

The USGS National Assessment of Coastal Change Hazards Project Extreme Storms and Hurricanes group thanks the many scientists and research assistants who have contributed to the research and data collections that made this assessment possible. We would especially like to acknowledge Abby Sallenger, who was instrumental in the creation and development of the National Assessment Coastal Change Hazards project. Extensive data processing and mapping support were provided by Kathryn Smith, Laura Fauver, Kristy Guy and Jolene Gittens. We also thank the EAARL and CHARTS programs as well as USGS field support and survey teams for the comprehensive lidar dataset that formed the basis of this analysis. Emily Himmelstoss and Peter Howd provided thorough and thoughtful reviews. This research has been supported by the USGS Coastal and Marine Geology Program.

References Cited

Holthuijsen, L.H., Booij, N., and Ris, R.C., 1993, A spectral wave model for the coastal zone, *in* Wiegel, R.L., Magoon, O.T., and Hemsley, J.M., eds., Ocean wave measurement and analysis: Proceedings of the Second International Symposium, honoring professor Robert L. Wiegel, New Orleans, Louisiana, July 25–28, 1993, p. 630–641.

Houston, S.H., Shaffer, W.A., Powell, M.D., and Chen, J., 1999, Comparisons of HRD and SLOSH surface wind fields in hurricanes: Implications for storm surge modeling: Weather and Forecasting, v. 14, p. 671–686.

Irish, J.L., Resio, D.T., and Ratcliff, J.J., 2008, The influence of storm size on hurricane surge: Journal of Physical Oceanography, v. 38, no. 9, p. 2003–2013.

Irish, J.L., Resio, D.T., and Cialone, M.A., 2009, A surge response function approach to coastal hazard assessment. Part 2: Quantification of spatial attributes of response functions: Natural Hazards, v. 51, no. 1, p. 183–205.

Jarvinen, B.R., and Lawrence, M.B., 1985, An evaluation of the SLOSH storm surge model: Bulletin of the American Meteorological Society, v. 66, no. 11, p. 1408–1411.

Le Treut, H., Somerville, R., Cubasch, U., Ding, Y., Mauritzen, C., Mokssit, A., Peterson, T., and Prather, M., 2007, Historical overview of climate change, in Climate Change 2007: The Physical Science Basis: Cambridge, Cambridge University Press.

Morgan, K.L.M., and Sallenger, A.H., Jr., 2009, Coastal change during Hurricane Isabel 2003: U.S. Geological Survey Fact Sheet 2009–3025, 2 p.

National Oceanic and Atmospheric Administration (NOAA), 2007, Hurricane preparedness: SLOSH model, National Hurricane Center.

Plant, N.G., Holland, K.T., and Puleo, J.A., 2002, Analysis of the scale of errors in nearshore bathymetric data: Marine Geology, v. 191, no. 1–2, p. 71–86.

Plant, N.G., and Stockdon, H.F., 2012, Probabilistic prediction of barrier-island response to hurricanes: Journal of Geophysical Research Earth Surface, v. 117, F03015, doi:10.1029/2011JF002326.

Plant, N.G., Stockdon, H.F., Sallenger, A.H., Jr., Turco, M.J., East, J.W., Taylor, A.A., and Shaffer, W.A., 2010, Forecasting hurricane impact on coastal topography: Eos Transactions American Geophysical Union, v. 91, no. 7, p. 65–66.

Sallenger, A.H., 2000, Storm impact scale for barrier islands: Journal of Coastal Research, v. 16, no. 3, p. 890–895.

Sallenger, A.H., Krabill, W., Swift, R., Brock, J., List, J., Hansen, M., Holman, R.A., Manizade, S., Sontag, J., Meredith, A., Morgan, K., and Stockdon, H., 2003, Evaluation of airborne scanning lidar for coastal change applications: Journal of Coastal Research, v. 19, p. 125–133.

Sallenger, A.H., Stockdon, H.F., Fauver, L.A., Hansen, M., Thompson, D.T., Wright, C.W., and Lillycrop, J., 2006, Hurricanes 2004: An overview of their characteristics and coastal change: Estuaries and Coasts, v. 29, no. 6A, p. 880–888.

Sallenger, A.H., Jr., Wright, C.W., Guy, K.K., and Morgan, K.L.M., 2004, Assessing storm-induced damage and dune erosion using airborne lidar: Examples from Hurricane Isabel: Shore & Beach, v. 72, no. 2, p. 3–7.

Sallenger, A.H., Jr., Wright, C.W., and Lillycrop, W.J., 2005, Coastal impacts of the 2004 hurricanes measured with airborne lidar; initial results: Shore and Beach, v. 73, no. 2&3, p. 10–14.

Stockdon, H.F., Doran, K.S., and Sallenger, A.H., 2009, Extraction of lidar-based dune-crest elevations for use in examining the vulnerability of beaches to inundation during hurricanes: Journal of Coastal Research, v. 25, no. 6, p. 59–65.

Stockdon, H.F., Doran, K.J., Thompson, D.M., Sopkin, K.L., Plant, N.G., and Sallenger, A.H., 2012, National assessment of hurricane-induced coastal erosion hazards—Gulf of Mexico: U.S. Geological Survey Open-File Report 2012–1084, 51 p., available at *http://pubs.usgs.gov/of/2012/1084/*.

Stockdon, H.F., Holman, R.A., Howd, P.A., and Sallenger, A.H., 2006, Empirical parameterization of setup, swash, and runup: Coastal Engineering, v. 53, no. 7, p. 573–588.

Stockdon, H.F., Sallenger, A.H., Holman, R.A., and Howd, P.A., 2007a, A simple model for the spatially-variable coastal response to hurricanes: Marine Geology, v. 238, p. 1–20.

Stockdon, H.F., Thompson, D.M., and Sallenger, A.H., 2007b, Hindcasting potential hurricane impacts on rapidly changing barrier islands, in Proceedings, Coastal Sediments '07: Sixth International Symposium on Coastal Engineering and Science of Coastal Sediment Processes, New Orleans, Louisiana, May 13–17, 2007, American Society of Civil Engineers, p. 976–985.

Tables

Table 1. Mean elevation of dune crest (z_c) and dune toe (z_t) and mean beach slope (β_m) for the sandy beaches along the southeast Atlantic coast. [Standard deviation is given in parentheses. m, meter]

State/region	z_c [m]	z_t [m]	β_m	Survey date [month/year]
U.S. southeast Atlantic coast	3.84 (1.40)	2.26 (0.69)	0.062 (0.029)	
Florida	4.71 (1.52)	2.72 (0.81)	0.082 (0.041)	8/2009, 5/2010
Georgia	3.28 (1.50)	2.16 (0.73)	0.041 (0.019)	5/2010
South Carolina	2.93 (0.85)	1.85 (0.46)	0.055 (0.029)	5/2010
North Carolina	4.44 (1.73)	2.29 (0.75)	0.054 (0.026)	8/2009, 5/2010

Table 2. Mean input wind speed, significant wave height (H_s), and wave period (T_p) and modeled setup (η_{setup}), runup (η_{R2}) and storm surge (η_{surge}) for category 1-5 hurricanes. [Standard deviation is given in parentheses. m, meter; m/s, meters per second; s, second]

Hurricane intensity category	Wind speed [m/s]	H_s [m]	T_p [s]	η_{setup} [m]	η_{R2} [m]	η_{surge} [m]
1	42.5	7.44 (0.28)	14.03 (0.41)	1.03 (0.50)	3.26 (0.94)	1.88 (0.63)
2	49.2	7.72 (0.20)	14.44 (0.30)	1.08 (0.52)	3.42 (0.97)	3.05 (0.95)
3	58.1	8.09 (0.14)	15.00 (0.22)	1.15 (0.55)	3.63 (1.02)	4.18 (1.19)
4	69.3	8.52 (0.11)	15.68 (0.18)	1.23 (0.59)	3.90 (1.09)	5.23 (1.40)
5	73.8	8.69 (0.11)	15.94 (0.18)	1.27 (0.60)	4.00 (1.12)	6.27 (1.57)

Table 3. Percentage of coast very likely ($p > 0.9$) to experience erosion associated with collision, overwash, and inundation during category 1–5 hurricanes.

	Hurricane intensity category				
	1	2	3	4	5
Collision					
U.S. southeast Atlantic coast	89	95	96	96	96
Florida	92	99	99	99	100
Georgia	98	100	100	100	100
South Carolina	100	100	100	100	100
North Carolina	91	99	100	100	100
Overwash					
U.S. southeast Atlantic coast	47	66	78	87	92
Florida	30	56	78	91	97
Georgia	71	89	95	97	97
South Carolina	96	99	100	100	100
North Carolina	31	52	65	78	89
Inundation					
U.S. southeast Atlantic coast	12	36	51	64	75
Florida	1	7	29	52	75
Georgia	40	68	84	93	95
South Carolina	34	95	99	100	100
North Carolina	4	23	39	50	59

www.ingramcontent.com/pod-product-compliance
Lightning Source LLC
Chambersburg PA
CBHW080347300526
45791CB00026B/2863